Fear:

The Wellness Workbook 1

Written & Un-Edited

by Darick Spears

Fear: The Wellness Workbook 1

ISBN: 978-1-954133-00-6

Copyright © 2020 by Darick Spears

Darick Books

All rights reserved. No part of this book may be reproduced or transmitted in any form or by any means without written permission from the author.

Published through

Darick Books

DDS MediaWorks LLC./21st Century Shakespears Publishing

www.darickbooks.com

Get Your Book Written & Published today By Darick Spears

Email: darick@ddsmediaworks.com

Call 414-988-4946

Meditations I	5
The Un-Knowing	9
Say it Loud	12
The Mirrors of Fear	15
Different Types of Phobias	19
Some Unusual Phobias	21
7 Common Fears	23
Acknowledging the Fear	25
The Necessary Evil	27
Stop	29
Fear Related Control	31
Facing the Fear	36
Look it In the Eye	39
Rollout	41
Notebook	43

Welcome to the first Book of wellness from Darick Books. This workbook will help you as the reader to deal with fear. The weight of fear can prevent you from the heights that you want to ascend to in life.

Learning to deal with fear is my approach within this book. I encourage you to answer the questions – and to be honest. We will get through these stages of fear together.

Peace and Love from your brother,

Darick Spears

Meditations I

Meditation 1

I will not let fear drive this car.

I will not let fear put any extra beats in my heart.

I am more than a half,

I am whole.

I am the one in the driver's seat,

But God is in control.

Fear will not stop me from driving this car,

I have the key in the ignition,

Foot on the pedal.

It's time to ride.

Meditation 2

I don't believe in running,

Unless it's to get ahead in this race.

I don't believe in hiding,

Unless it's to put my head down to pick up my pace.

Fear will not get the best of me.

Fear can only be my fuel.

Fear will not be the weight that holds me down,

Faith is the cure.

One step,

One focus,

One road to my final destination.

Fear is just an illusion,

It's time for my elevation.

Meditation 3

Why am I afraid to walk up this dark staircase?

I see the light at the top.

Why do I see the first step and hesitate?

Why am I afraid to try?

Is it because I know that a change is near?

A change that is for the best.

Is it because the thought of success presents me with fear?

Is fear what causes the shadows on the stairs?

Why am I afraid to reach the top of the staircase?

I see the light at the top.

This time I will not hesitate,

My faith shall see me out.

The Un-Knowing

(Note from Author)

Fear

Do you know that most times fear comes from the unknowing—when we are not sure about something, we tend to become fearful. A great way to get over your fear is to become knowledgeable about what it is that is making you afraid. Sometimes, we are scared to take that leap of faith because we don't understand the capacity of the leap.

The leap could lead you to firm ground or no ground at all: and this causes the fear. But the courage to have faith in whatever you choose to do will eliminate the fear.

When I first started writing books, one of my biggest fears was that I would not ever be able to publish it—unless I got with a huge publishing company.

But as I began to research, and gain knowledge—I found out that I could self-publish my own books. That eliminated my fears in the publishing world. That's just one example of how I found a way to eliminate my fear. They say fear is an illusion—and I have to agree in several ways. This is because when we find it hard to understand something—we make up things in our head that are really not reality.

Say It Loud

Today I want you to recite these phrases out loud.

1. I deserve the best

2. I am the best at what I do.

3. I have the ability to become very wealthy.

4. I will walk through the door of opportunity without hesitation.

5. I believe in myself and my ability to change the world around me for the better.

6. I am not a failure -- I am a walking billboard of success.

7. If I can think it, then it can be done.

8. I am a failure if I choose not to try.

9. I am beautiful inside and out.

When you reinforce yourself with positive, you will get positive in return. On the next page, I want you to be true to yourself and write down the fears that challenge you at this moment in your life.

The Mirrors of Fear

What are Your Present Fears?

1. _____

2. _____

3. _____

4. _____

5. _____

6. _____

7. _____

8. _____

9. _____

Below write down why you fear these things?

If you find yourself unsure of why you fear certain things – then you should consider pinpointing what makes you unsure. This could be the reason that you are full of fear. Being unaware of something seizes the mind with fear.

If you took a wrong turn into a dark alley, the threat of possibility, will riot the fear inside of your veins. This is because you are unsure of what the dark alley has instore for you.

Could it be a group of pirates waiting to digest your gold? Or could it be a rat with bad breath excited about meeting you face to face? Fear derives from uncertainty – but the more understanding you obtain the less impact the fear has.

Different Types of Phobias

1. Acrophobia
   - fear of heights
2. Aerophobia
   - fear of flying
3. Arachnophobia
   - fear of spiders
4. Astraphobia
   - fear of thunder and lightning
5. Autophobia
   - fear of being alone
6. Claustrophobia
   - fear of confined or crowded spaces
7. Hemophobia
   - fear of blood
8. Hydrophobia
   - fear of water
9. Ophidiophobia
   - fear of snakes
10. Zoophobia
    - fear of animals

Some Unusual Phobias

(Author's Note)

There are many fears that people hold on to. Here are a few unusual ones.

1. Alektorophobia-
    - fear of chickens
2. Onomatophobia
    - fear of names
3. Pogonophobia
    - fear of beards
4. Nephophobia
    - fear of clouds
5. Cryophobia
    - fear of ice or cold

7

Common

Fears

1. Fear of criticism.

2. Fear of poverty

3. Fear of old age (and death)

4. Fear of failure

5. Fear of offending others

6. Fear of looking foolish

7. Fear of success

Acknowledging the Fear

Meditation 4

I acknowledge the fears in my life,

I only know them to exist,

But they will not stop me from completing my goals.

I acknowledge the fears in my life,

I only know them to exist,

But they will not affect my positive attitude towards life.

I thank God for my new opportunities,

I thank him for the courage.

I thank him for the wisdom to dip my feet into the waters of

riches.

I acknowledge the fears in my life,

I only know them to exist,

But the fears in my life – today, I simply will dismiss.

The Necessary Evil

Fear is not always a bad thing. This is because fear can be a tool of caution. When you are walking into a new place – fear can be the balance that bridges together your curiosity and suspicion.

(Author's Note)

Stop!

Right now!

If you are thinking about giving up, then you need to STOP.

See it all of the way through.

You will not fail.

Success is right around the corner. Sometimes we get more and more afraid when we are near new heights.

Elevation can feel awkward – turbulence is a factor during elevation: but your new level is HERE.

Giving up is NOT AN OPTION.

Always finish what you start.

Fear related to Control

While it is only natural to feel fear when you have no control – please know that what you cannot control you should not fear. When you have done all that you can in any situation – then be content and wait for the results.

You will get what you desire in the end; and it will all work out in your favor. When God blesses us with something, all we have to do is reach out and grasp it. Holding on to it – can embody the high amount of work that you must put in to having it.

It may take some late nights or early mornings – but the work you put into your blessing shows how much you appreciate it.

For example, if God blesses you with a new house – you must put work into its upkeep. If you don't cut the grass, clean the house, and other factors of upkeep- then it could go to shambles.

Fear and control are cousins – but it is best that they stay distant.

"Fear of man will prove to be a snare, but whoever trusts in the Lord is kept safe."

~ Proverbs 29:25

Meditation 5

Whom shall I fear except God?

Who believes in me more than myself?

The light that I have in me will not be blanketed.

I will get through my storm.

Whom shall I fear?

The simple answer is no one.

Facing the Fear

Write down ways that you vow to face your fears.

1. _____

2. _____

3. _____

4. _____

5. _____

6. _____

7. _____

8. _____

9. _____

10. _____

11. _____

What are some ways that you can improve your way of thinking? Are you always negative? Are you always looking for the worst in every situation? Today I want you to be positive – write down some positive outcomes that you see happening in your path and future.

1. _____

2. _____

3. _____

4. _____

5. _____

6. _____

7. _____

8. _____

9. _____

Look It in The Eye

It is about that time. You must face your fear(s). Imagine your worst fear(s) and embrace it(them). Stare at it eye to eye – feel it in your veins. Now release it. I want you to notice something, and that is – you looked your worst fear in its face, and you are still here. You were not destroyed. When you learn to face your fears then you become stronger. The fear becomes smaller and your confidence grows.

When I first decided to leave my parent's house- 2 weeks after my high school graduation to attend my first year in college: I was frightened. I was the first to attend College from my household, and my worst fear was that I would fail my classes, not be able to afford school -- and end up a homeless person (with no disrespect to homeless people.) While I feared those things, I also feared that if I didn't try, I would regret it for the rest of my life.

I had no clue that I would end up getting my Associates, Bachelor's, and my Master's Degree, before age 29. I could have never imagined that— but I took the chance and faced my fears. It wasn't easy, but I didn't let fear stop me from trying.

So, remember, when you learn to face your fears -- you also add a layer of maturity and strength to your life and journey. Face it.

RoLLOut

This book was not intended to be super long and boring. Rather, I wanted it to be short, powerful, and effective. Use this as a workbook for yourself – a guide to assist you in overcoming your fears in life.

Fear is not always a bad thing. But it can be very detrimental if you let it prevent you from reaching your fullest potential. I wish you much success on your journey and I hope that you accomplish more goals than you can imagine.

God bless you my friend.

Much love and success,

From Your Brother – Darick Spears

Notebook

www.ingramcontent.com/pod-product-compliance
Lightning Source LLC
Chambersburg PA
CBHW081206170426
43197CB00018B/2935